iLearn, iTeach

Kathrine Yets

Cyberwit.net
HIG 45 Kaushambi Kunj, Kalindipuram
Allahabad - 211011 (U.P.) India
http://www.cyberwit.net
Tel: +(91) 9415091004
E-mail: info@cyberwit.net

Printed at Repro India Limited.

Acknowledgements

I would like to thank my poetry mentors Margaret Rozga, Alison Townsend, Marrilyn Annucci, Michael Belongie, and others along the way. Special thanks to Jim Landwehr and Nick Pedriana for their specific and caring critiques over the years. A warm thank you as always to Kathie Giorgio and her workshop studio AllWriters'. And the biggest of hugs to my fellow teachers and the students who I have worked with.

Contents

iLearn, iTeach 1

During the War 8

When I Was 13 9

Today 11

Damn 12

Swimming in Thunder 13

Trouble 14

Ray 15

Little Me 16

High on a Tuesday 17

All Your Buttons 18

Weed of My Loins 20

She Doesn't 22

My Mother's Lover 23

Joist 24

Unlove 25

iTeach 27

Creative Congestion 28

Learning Figurative Language 29

Learning Haiku 30

Teacher's Favorite 31

iLearn, iTeach 32

Theme 33

Craw 34

Avoiding 35

Teacher Daze 36

Meeting the Parents 37

My Zombies 38
An A 39
The Little One 40
Journals 41
Resignation 43
You Asked What is Wrong 44
Love Was Not Enough 45
Recognitions 46

iLearn

During the War

inspired by Brittany Sanchez's photography

Spring had left us restless like crocuses crouched in the grass.
The sound of airplanes brought us home every night,
rustling through the backyard to a wet porch
floodlit by the kitchen window. The sky a washed-out denim,
stalling before the stars came. We stumbled
up the wood steps, and the whoosh above
made us cover our ears. We were young,
and our eyes rolled up like in death to look.
We were young and knew nothing of disaster
or a longing for home. We were always home.
Could smell our stepdad's vodka before it hit the glass.
The planes flew just above our roof
so close we thought we could just reach and grab a wing.

When I Was 13

"That little guy? Don't worry about that little guy."
~Super Troopers

Life was a marijuana smoke cloud.
Boys were all I thought about.
I might have wrote a poem or two
or an entire full length collection
all about love
and weed
and suicide.
When I was thirteen,
I was prescribed a lot of drugs.
They said I was *manic*.
I was a maniac
with a Nintendo 64 controller.
I was Saturdays swinging at the park.
I was smoking in the girl's bathroom.
I was...
I don't recall.
But I was everywhere,
rollercoastering on shrooms
into the couch.
I was pill popping,
waking up two days later than I expected.
I was drinking flat Coronas in my basement.
I was too good for my own bad,
but man, I had no worries
of where I could lay my head
or get my next bowl

of cereal.
I was young
and still am.
Over a decade later,
life is filled with white space,
waiting to be filled,
and I am writing poems
about a life that seems so distant
but was mine.

Today

Beyond the geranium boulevards,
blocks from Sendik's Food Market

rain falls on tin roofs
and twinbed park benches,

a dead kitten on the roadside.
It's always partly cloudy.

Mondays smell like macaroni
and feel like jump-ropes hitting your ankles.

Splash, pitter patter, thump
in the streets of puddles.

Damn

Damn, I said at age five.
Damn because my friend's dad died.
Damn because I missed the funeral.
Damn was my dad mad I said damn.
Damn, did that spanking hurt.
Damn is a bad word; I learned.

Swimming in Thunder

I was young, swimming in a grey sky
lit every now and again with bright yellow.
I was young and knew nothing of today—
nothing beyond the church steeples and playground
with the yellow horses swinging.
I knew how to swim, and did I swim,
despite the lifeguards yelling between the booms.
I was young and knew nothing of science and reason
or hurt and pain beside a scratch on my leg
and third degree burn on my foot.
There was no tomorrow, only the possibility of the moment
in that pool of blue/green chlorine
that I can still taste
and the thunder still ringing through me.

Trouble

Trouble
they called me as I grabbed the swirling blue
bong from makeshift table covered in burns.
Trouble
they called me when I kissed
more than one boy in a day.
Trouble
they called me when I walked down the road
at two in the morning in mini jean skirt.
Trouble
they called me.

Ray

A name like neon bar lights and Sprite on the tongue—fizzle.
A name that pushes me back to preteen spin-the-bottle
first (or second?) kiss.
The "What Would Raymond Do?" mentality
of my middle school years,
trying so hard to be like the boy next door.
He so kool, I thought to myself as smoke swirled in the air
and my stick legs dangled off the porch swing.

Ray— the boy my mother warned me about.
Cars dismantled on the front lawn and dirt bike
jumps piled high off to the side.
"That Raymond… That Barnes boy…" my mother would say
and blame him for another one of my drunken
teen mistakes even though he was usually never there.

What am I trying to say?
All this from a name—motor engine rolling off the tongue.
I cannot roll my [r]'s but when I say that name,
his name, it feels just the same.

Little Me

To past friends, Kathrine is a cacophony;
they want to squish me down: Katie.
Back to rainbows and macaroni—
the tiny ie of childhood,
electric-sliding to teen years.
Stop, step back, shimmy forward.
Kathrine is not "too old"—
a ripe honeydew—pure
as a communion wafer
soaked in wine.

High on a Tuesday

Is that God?
Over there, next to the burnt toast?
A deity beyond me, above me,
beside me. I have been personifying
this almighty vapor, air of existence,
for years. I have grown bored.
Bored of floating. Bored of what is to come.
The end is near, they say.
The end is here.

All Your Buttons

I'll let you try on a marriage skirt,
a skirt with all your buttons, all your beliefs,
he told me drunk one night last spring.
He has no idea what he meant.

He claims to not be an alcoholic,
but I wonder if he was in a previous life
since he always craves but nothing fills

which reminds me of a time I was high
and was thoroughly convinced I stepped in roadkill.
The sun made me squint, and my flip flops
hit heavy on the asphalt. I saw the rabbit.
I retched under the Maple Street bridge.

This connects somehow. I felt so empty
despite my lungs being filled after Holly
passed me the pipe, and Gabby,
who would die about a decade later,
laughed with her fire engine hair
whipping up around her.

All your buttons. All your beliefs.
Then, I believed in nothing but pink wildflowers
that would turn purple when grazed slightly by a cigarette cherry.
I believed friendship lived forever next to an old abandoned barn.
I believed in something when Gabby rode horses.

But this is all a bottle of literature I drank years ago.

Now, I drink wine and smoke Mavericks.
Now, I see Gabby's face reconstructed after the accident
inside a casket.
Now, Holly has a baby.
Now, I'm wearing a marriage skirt and watching
my boyfriend drink vodka from our mason cups.

Weed of My Loins

It's hard to focus when her subconscious
is always looking for a mother.
What about the woman with the azalea bushes?
A feminine pink with a twisted trunk, bushy tops remind her
of her mother's blouse, which she wore during her manic episode.
Run.

You know there's a problem when she's eating popsicles in the
bathroom.
When the hair dryer's cord isn't
wrapped and sprawled out near the sink.
Her mother doesn't notice. Her mother has her own hair dryer.

Almost met the goal of never screaming like her mother.
2015, she locks herself in the bathroom and turns on the fan.
Looks in the mirror and wonders where she has been.
She screams.

In a world where Google is her mother,
and she can't judge a good cantaloupe,
she decides it's best to give up on unconditional love, that thing
with pink blooms
bursting open only with the seasons. With spring. Within the
spring she was three years old
and her mother took her, foot on the gas, trying to save them from…
Maybe her father. From the dangers of loving too much or too little.

But they forgot about the sister. Forgot her and the mother had to turn.
To go to church. To find a pastor in wolves' clothing. To find

you can't run from love. That running from love meant she was crazy.
The daughters visited their mother in the mental hospital,
surrounded by plumes of cigarette smoke.

Twenty years later, and she still hears her mother's scream.
Remembers turning on the church bathroom fan by accident
and her mother screaming like knives. She cries and still asks
on car rides *where are we going?*
where are we going? between deep breaths.

What is happiness to you? she keeps asking friends and strangers,
blowing cigarette smoke into the void of avoided answers.
She asks her mother even though she knows the answer:
driving in the car with her daughter, windows down, sun shining.

She Doesn't

I don't want to die,
my mother says
after a round of Bloody Mary's.
It is midnight
a week before her surgery.
Before laser meets skin.
I tell her she doesn't have to.
She can live forever.

My Mother's Lover

When I hear the Ghostbusters' theme song,
I can't help but cry, thinking of you standing
in front of the television all medicationed out,
laughing. I remember. How you watched
the movie every night for two months.
Your ashes still float down the Ohio River.
Your songs still play in my head.
"You'll never be the same," you sang,
and you're right.

Joist

My father fastened the joists of pine for our deck. The sun was setting, and I twirled a blue lace parasol. Does he know one day he will lock my mother out of the house— she would pound and pound on the sliding glass door while I didn't ask why. That day, far away. Then, there was joy. There was joy.

Unlove

My father's eyes pool behind
John Lennon glasses.
Your mother did not love me.
On a bench off the bank of the Fox,
sun sets like a cliché,
hyacinth pinks and purples,
some gray. *She did not love me,*
he says and goes on,
tears pearling on his cheeks,
and I learn what love isn't.
I learn where to go when I'm lonely—
this river edge, these rocks.
How to wrap memories in newspaper
and keep them in a box.

iTeach

Creative Congestion

An infection in my soul
Chakras out of sync
The colors palid
Where did my rainbow go?
Submerged in mucus
Create an incision in my occipital lobe
Get to the center of the sense
Lobotomize me
Put William Blake's brain in there
Sizzle it around a bit with a fire iron
 hot poker
Not the flower
Or yes, the flower——
Swirl blooms around my cranium
And maybe I will become visceral.

Learning Figurative Language

His small hands
hold pencil and penguin eraser.
Adolescent, pubescent, intelligent
Eyes analyze similes—
A taco is like…
Personification: Kevin.
Rhyme: He came from heaven.
Metaphor is an ocean
he drowns in.
Makes him feel dumb as a donkey.
Hyperbole.
Touch his shoulder
tell him he is a lion
or an owl or an elephant,
so he never forgets
how amazing he is.

Learning Haiku

You ask your students to write haikus,
they put dashes between each word—
each line beats the syllable
5
7
5
punctuated.
The haikus are in your chest today
beneath the jasper stone
sewing your tendineae together—
coughing their words—
enriched with their ideas.

Teacher's Favorite

You ran to my room crying
when another teacher embarrassed you.
I played Marshmello and Bastille,
and it did make you happier.
I gave you a concealer to cover your puffy eyes.
I wanted to tell you I loved you,
and everything would be okay
today, tomorrow, and the next day,
but I think you knew.

iLearn, iTeach

I was once you,
high as fuck
sitting in a desk
wondering when it will be over
so I can go smoke more.

I was once you,
not worried about tomorrow
but rather how Jeni
was mad at me for
kissing her ex next to a gravestone.

I was once you,
not knowing or caring
about prepositions and paragraphs,
mind maps,
but I loved my own photograph
and would look at myself for hours.

I was once you,
uncertain about my future
so I jazzed June in the moment
living young.
Immature tongue.

Theme

Once you compare theme to prom,
they start to somewhat understand.
Do you go to an ocean themed prom
dressed as a fish or mermaid?
NO.
It is more subtle than that.
When Paravana chops off her hair,
this can relate to what thematic concept?
Bravery, Michael said.
What could be the thematic statement?
Not a peep.

Craw

Christ forgive them, for they know not.
A metaphor does not have like or as.
A flashlight is not a flashlight;
it's a snake that glows.
Personification is a human blowing their nose…
No no no.
If I read one more analysis of Katy Perry's
"Firework," I'm going to explode
into twenty different colors in the sky.
You are the first person to think
the ocean is full of angel tears.
You are the only one who knows
we are capable of so much more.
You craw like a crow without a throat
about that sad song.
You're a new song, baby.
Now write a new song.
And stop saying like like that.
It's not a simile until
you make a comparison
like a poet.
You're not a poet
until you suffer more than Mary,
watching her son die— false.
Stop dying for your own sins already.
Just write the damn poem.

Avoiding

I just watched one hour of videos on how to make cakes.
My hair is curled almost by single strands.
Outfits picked for the next two weeks.
Snapchat filters of bunny face with eyes enlarged.
I'm beautiful.
Discovering the perfect combination of Kool Aid and sugar.
What does my eye color mean?
Google. Google. Google.
Scroll my wall.
Wash my walls.
That picture on the wall looks crooked.
Straighten.
I have 500 emails, and 75% are ads,
20% newsletters,
5% students asking me to grade their papers…
Should probably do that.
After I watch this cat video.

Teacher Daze

That is not what I said.
That is not what I meant at all.
I don't have the time.
Screaming and my lessons.
Lesson plans.
Lessons of life
I will check tomorrow.
I have only graded the complex and compound assignment.
Lord help me.
Lord help with my students.
Help us.
Today is not feeling good.
Yesterday is not feeling well.
Correction.
Correction.
Correction.
Stop emailing me.
I'll do it tomorrow.
I promise.
But then I fall asleep.

Meeting the Parents

How am I not going to say
your child is a little shiitake mushroom.
while smiling my nice pearly smile.
Your scholar is not the brightest Crayola
and made me get gray hairs last week, literally,
when I saw the final.
Instead I say,
Your scholar could improve scores by doing…
 Everything he is supposed to be doing but is not.
I want to rip pillows apart and scream.
What I have to say is,
You child is such a great kid, but…
But I want to wap him in the head with a book.
Help my hair.
Help my sanity.
Stop the madness.

My Zombies

My creativity consumed by my students.
Like worms they work their way into
my skull as I try to mull over their ways—-
in a daze they sit for days on end without answers.
 What was said? What was said?
Scoop my brain out with their ladles.
Our zombies are so very active.
Attractive, even, with their shiny Jordans
and long polished nails.
If only they had purpose, meaning beyond their own images.
Selfies and video chats, looking in their mirrors
without reflection.

An A

Whenever you begin your story with *once upon a time*…
I want to smack your face with a dictionary.

Whenever you start by saying *like*…
and it is not a simile,
I want to shit on every English journal ever written.

Whenever you tell me a story about love
I want to castrate a pigeon in your face.

I don't know where you came from.
I don't know if this message will ever get to you.
Know I tried my best to teach you something
other than how to get an A.

The Little One

Ms. Yets hates me,
but I LOOOOVE HERRRRR!
she would sing out to the class.
She would tell me how naughty the class was
and how thick I was getting.
She swore like a bartender.
I put her right next to her bestie
because they would walk across the room
to see each other anyways.
I cannot express what you mean to me, child.
I do hate you,
but… nevermind.

Journals

I read all your journals.
Every. Damn. One.
All 76.
And let me tell you,
some of you are stupid as bong glass,
but most of you know more than you let on.
Tell me again what loves means
and trust and honesty.
How your words are sleek with poetry
and wisdom beyond your youth.
Tell me about that time your friends
deserted you and all you had was God.
Tell me your secrets, and I will hold them forever.

Resignation

It all comes down to an email.
You're not welcome back without a letter,
explaining your illness.
You're not welcome back
without opening up your skull
and showing them how your dopamine
doesn't flow just right
and how someone stuck a sizzling
iron to all your hopes and dreams,
swirling it around until it's soup.
You cannot show them a simple sickness.
You cannot show them the path from
your mental health to physical.
Because, sweetheart, it's all in your head.
And they could care less.
Unless you figure out how to put your words and thoughts
onto your skin like blisters or a rash
that would cover your whole body like constellations uncovering
your destructive ideation.
Still they would not understand
how scary it can be to leave the bedroom
or how hard it can be to lift your head.
You can't quite put your finger on it.
Your every thought a scuttling spider.
Explain to them this metaphor and what then?
Your resignation. Your death certificate.
Your only hope for a normal life imploded by a signature.
Signing off your sanity.
In the midst of your best self

you lost yourself once again
despite cutting off your own ears
to ignore the whispers of desperation
that you're not okay.
You're not okay.

You Asked What is Wrong

De: down,
away

Something keeps her sleeping,
weighs down her lids and begs to dream.
But no—she closes her eyes and only hears raindrops
and wakes to a cold sweat at 3 am. She sleepwalks
all day and can't control her silences.

press: to weigh heavily upon;
to compress or squeeze;
to alter in shape or size

Her torso bends, contorts forward
like a wilting petal curls in. She squeezes
between grocery aisles and sees products instead of faces.
She feels as small as an orange but not as vibrant.

ion: condition of,
result of,
act of,
process of,
state of

She is a charcoal portrait, stagnant pose
without purpose. Her arm hangs forward in inept plié
or she reaches, fingers splayed, for the sun.

Love Was Not Enough

You hug me, and my heart sings
the Pokemon theme song,
taking me back to my own childhood
and how I longed for an adult
to love me like a child should be.

I love you all like a mourning dove,
cooing late noon outside my patio door
like a lily opening fresh on my kitchen table.
I love you so much I had to leave you,
so you could grow big and strong and smart.

You were my world.
I woke up waiting to see you.
But I also spent days in bed worrying
that I was not good enough for you,
that my love was not enough
to show you how special you are.

Recognitions

"Avoiding" *Work Literary Magazine*

"During the War" Woodland Patterns April Poetry

"Resignation" *HerStry*

"Weed of My Loins" *The Blue Nib*